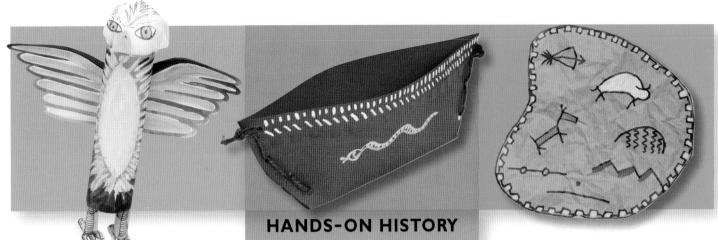

NATIVE NORTH AMERICANS

DRESS, EAT, WRITE, AND PLAY JUST LIKE THE NATIVE NORTH AMERICANS

JOE FULLMAN

QEB Publishing

Published in the United States by
QEB Publishing, Inc.
3 Wrigley, Suite A
Irvine, CA 92618

www.qeb-publishing.com

Library of Congress Cataloging-in-Publication Data

Fullman, Joe.
  Native North Americans : dress, eat, write, and play just like the Native Americans / Joe Fullman.
      p. cm. -- (QEB hands-on history)
  Includes index.
  ISBN 978-1-59566-245-3 (hardcover)
 1. Indians of North America--Study and teaching (Elementary)--Activity programs. 2. Indians of North America--History--Study and teaching (Elementary)--Activity programs. I. Title.
  E76.6.F85 2010
  973.04'97--dc22

                                    2009001115

Printed and bound
in China

Author Joe Fullman
Consultant John Malam
Editor Ben Hubbard
Designer Lisa Peacock
Project Maker Veronica Lenz

Publisher Steve Evans
Creative Director Zeta Davies
Managing Editor Amanda Askew

!

**TAKE CARE
WHEN USING SCISSORS**

Words in **bold** are
explained in the glossary
on page 30.

CONTENTS

WHO WERE THE NATIVE NORTH AMERICANS?

The Native North Americans were the first people to live in North America. They arrived about 15,000 years ago during the **Ice Age**. At that time, people living in Siberia walked across a bridge of land to the northwest tip of North America. Eventually they split themselves into many different **tribes**, such as the Apache, the Cheyenne and the Dakota.

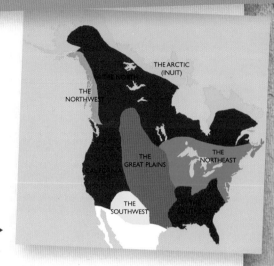

This map shows the areas where Native North American tribes lived. ▶

DID YOU KNOW?

THE FIRST PEOPLE TO ARRIVE IN NORTH AMERICA HUNTED GIANT ANIMALS, SUCH AS WOOLLY MAMMOTHS. THESE WERE A TYPE OF GIANT ELEPHANT WITH FURRY BODIES. WOOLLY MAMMOTHS DIED OUT AFTER THE END OF THE ICE AGE.

THE EUROPEANS ARRIVE

When the Ice Age ended about 10,000 years ago, water levels rose and Siberia became cut off from North America. No new people would arrive for thousands of years. Eventually, in the 16th century AD, European explorers came to North America. Over the next few centuries, lots of European people moved there.

This animal-shaped water pitcher was made by the Anasazi people more than 1,000 years ago. ▶

A Native North American performs a traditional dance at a **powwow**. ▶

CLOTHES

Throughout North America, the native tribes made their clothes from animal skins. They decorated their clothes using paints from plants and with objects, such as feathers and wampum beads. On their feet they wore moccasins, a type of shoe made from soft leather.

MAKE A WAMPUM BEAD BRACELET

Many North American tribes made pieces of jewelry called wampum beads from colored pieces of shell.

YOU WILL NEED

SMALL PASTA TUBES
RED FOOD DYE • STRING
RUBBING ALCOHOL • PENCIL
PLASTIC BAG • PLATE
SCISSORS • THIN CARDSTOCK
RUBBER GLOVES • GLUE

1 In a plastic bag, cover half the pasta with rubbing alcohol and 3 drops of food dye. Leave to dry on a plate.

2 On a piece of cardstock, draw a grid of 11 pasta shapes by 5 pasta shapes. Darken half the squares, as shown.

3 Cut 5 pieces of string, each twice as long as the grid. Thread the pasta onto the strings.

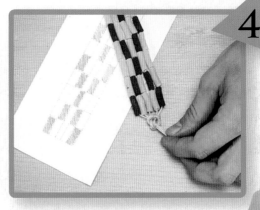

4 Make sure the order of the pasta matches the order on your grid. Tie knots in the ends of the strings.

5 Cut out the grid. Stick the strings of pasta onto the grid. Use the string to attach the bracelet to your arm.

Wampum beads were very valuable and were sometimes used as money. ▶

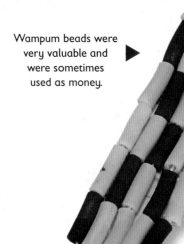

DIFFERENT LANDS, DIFFERENT PEOPLES

By the **16th century** AD, there were more than 300 Native North American tribes living in North America. These tribes had different ways of life, depending on where they lived. In the cold north, the people were **nomads**, following and hunting huge herds of **caribou**. In the forests of the northeast, the people farmed the land and lived in permanent settlements. In the central plains the tribes hunted buffalo, while in the dusty deserts of the southwest, the people lived in villages made of stone and clay.

◀ In southwestern deserts, people used sand to create magical, healing pictures.

INDIANS
Native North Americans are sometimes known as "American Indians." This is because the first Europeans to arrive in America thought they had found Asia, or the "Indies," as they were called. Today, most Native North Americans like to be called by their tribal name, such as Cherokee or Navajo. In Canada, the native tribes call themselves "First Nation" people.

DID YOU KNOW?
SOME NATIVE NORTH AMERICAN TRIBES USED FACE PAINT TO EXPRESS EMOTIONS. RED MEANT LIFE AND HAPPINESS, BLACK MEANT DEATH AND SADNESS, WHITE MEANT PEACE, AND YELLOW MEANT JOY.

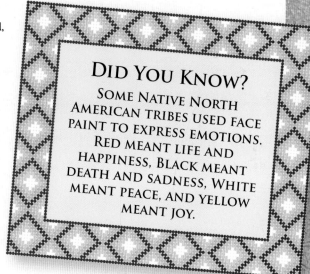

DIFFERENT LANGUAGES
The Native North American tribes spoke more than 200 languages. These languages were so different that many tribes could not talk to each other. Instead, they would use sign language to communicate.

◀ Native North Americans used sign language to communicate with each other and foreign settlers.

MAKE A NAVAJO SAND PAINTING

Healers from the Navajo tribe made paintings using colored sand. It was believed that these paintings had the power to cure illnesses.

YOU WILL NEED

COLORED SAND • GLUE • PAPER
PLASTIC CONTAINERS (SUCH AS
YOGURT CONTAINERS) • PENCIL

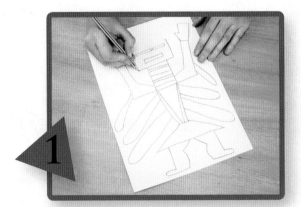

1

Half fill each container with colored sand. Draw a design on the paper.

2

Number shapes that are going to be the same color. Spread the glue into the shapes of color number 1.

3

Cover your paper with the sand that matches color number 1.

4

Lift the paper and carefully shake off the excess.

5

Repeat for each of the colors, then leave to dry.

▶ You can use any colors to create your sand painting.

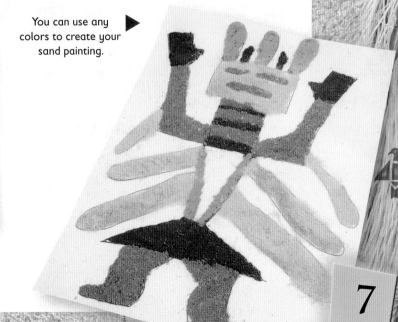

7

THE SPIRIT WORLD

Native North American tribes believed that the natural world was controlled by the Spirit World. The Native North Americans **worshipped** these spirits and performed **ceremonies** to ask for their help. To ask for guidance from the spirits, a ceremony called the Sun Dance was performed. Another ceremony, called the Rain Dance, asked for more rain. Religious leaders, called shamans, were in charge of the ceremonies. Shamans wore costumes and animal-shaped masks.

The dream catcher has a net to let good dreams through and keep bad ones out.

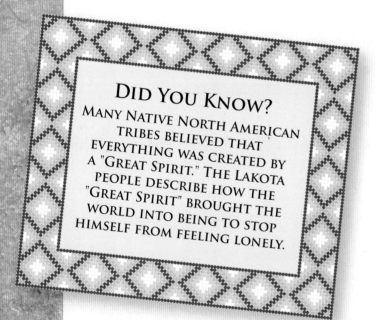

DID YOU KNOW?
MANY NATIVE NORTH AMERICAN TRIBES BELIEVED THAT EVERYTHING WAS CREATED BY A "GREAT SPIRIT." THE LAKOTA PEOPLE DESCRIBE HOW THE "GREAT SPIRIT" BROUGHT THE WORLD INTO BEING TO STOP HIMSELF FROM FEELING LONELY.

SHAMANS
Shamans were very important people in Native North American society. They were believed to be able to communicate with the spirits of the Spirit World. Shamans also acted as the tribe's doctor. If a member of the tribe was ill, the shaman would perform a ceremony to drive the sickness, or "evil spirit," from their body. Shamans would hang a dream catcher above a child's bed to prevent nightmares.

EUROPEAN DISEASES
Native North Americans used medicines made from herbs and plants to cure illnesses. Unfortunately, these did not work against diseases brought to North America by Europeans. Hundreds of thousands of Native North Americans died from measles and chicken pox. The Europeans were naturally **immune** to these diseases, but the Native North Americans were not.

Shamans carried their medicines in bags that were decorated with beads. ▶

MAKE A DREAM CATCHER

Dream catchers were invented by the Ojibwa tribe. They have become popular throughout the Native North American world.

YOU WILL NEED
PAIR OF COMPASSES • PENCIL
COLORED CARDSTOCK
SCISSORS • HOLE PUNCH • STRING
STICKY TAPE • COLORED BEADS
PAINTBRUSH AND PAINTS
LARGE WHITE CARDSTOCK

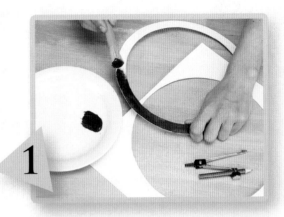

1 Use compasses to draw and cut out a ring of cardstock, 12 in (30 cm) by 1 in (3 cm). Paint and leave to dry.

2 Make 12 holes in the ring 1 in (2.5 cm) apart. Thread and tape a piece of string through one of the holes.

3 Add two beads to the string. Thread the end through a hole in the opposite side of the ring. Tie a knot.

4 Repeat with more string to create a web. Cut some cardstock feather shapes.

5 Tape long pieces of string to the bottom of the catcher. Add beads and colored feathers on the ends.

Hang your dream catcher above your bed to stop bad dreams from getting in. ▶

WARFARE

Tribes often fought each other using bows, arrows, and war clubs. As more people arrived from Europe, the tribes began to join together to fight against the settlers. They also began to use new weapons brought over by the Europeans, such as guns. Successful warriors sometimes wore eagle feather headdresses to show their importance.

Tribes hunted in the forests using axes called tomahawks. ▶

MAKE A WARRIOR HEADDRESS

Large headdresses were worn only in open areas where there were no trees for them to get caught on.

Eagle feather headdresses were also known as "war bonnets." ▼

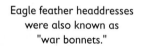

YOU WILL NEED
BAND OF CORRUGATED CARDBOARD, 14 IN (35 CM) BY 2 IN (6 CM) • PAINTBRUSH AND PAINTS • SCISSORS • HOLE PUNCH • TWO LONG PIECES OF RIBBON • STICKY TAPE • COLORED CARDSTOCK

1

Paint one side of the corrugated cardboard band with patterns.

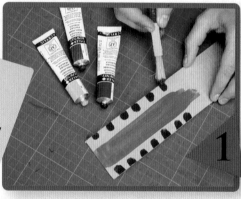

3

Tuck the feathers into the holes at the top of the band. Use sticky tape to keep them in place.

10

THE TRIBES UNITE

In the 18th century, six of the most powerful tribes in North America joined together to fight. They called themselves the League of Iroquois. The league won many battles, but was eventually forced to give up most of its lands.

THE PEACE PIPE

Many Native North Americans smoked tobacco, which they believed had healing powers. Some tribes celebrated the end of a war by smoking tobacco in a **calumet**, or peace pipe. The leaders of the tribes would sit in a circle, taking puffs from the pipe.

The Iroquois chief, "Cornplanter," holding a calumet. ▶

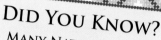

DID YOU KNOW?
MANY NATIVE NORTH AMERICANS HAD TATTOOS ON THEIR BODY TO SHOW WHICH TRIBE THEY BELONGED TO.

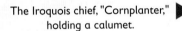

Using different colored cardstock, cut out 12 feather shapes.

Tie the headdress to your head with the ribbon. ▶

Punch a hole at each end of the band. Thread a piece of ribbon through each hole and tie in a knot.

11

LIFE IN THE NORTHEAST

In many parts of North America, the native tribes moved from place to place following great herds of animals, which they hunted. However, in the northeast, people farmed the fertile soils and built permanent homes. The tribes hunted animals in the forests, such as deer, using bows, arrows, and stone axes. They also fished in the sea and lakes, often using canoes.

Tribes fought using sharp axes called tomahawks, which they sometimes threw at each other.

The men of the tribe built the longhouses, while the women prepared the food.

LONGHOUSES

The most common house in northeast North America was called a "longhouse," which was made from long wooden poles covered in bark. A longhouse could be up to 165 feet (50 meters) long and divided into several living spaces. A dozen families might live in one longhouse.

Native North Americans used paddles to move and steer their canoes on lakes and rivers.

BOUNTIFUL FORESTS

The forests of the northeast provided the local tribes with many of their basic needs. Wood was used to build tools, weapons, and the frames of houses. Bark from birch trees was cut and sewn together using tree roots to make roofs, barrels, and canoes.

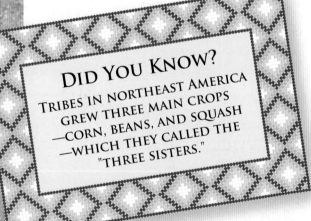

MAKE A NATIVE AMERICAN CANOE

Native North American canoes were light and easy to move, but they could carry very heavy loads.

YOU WILL NEED
LARGE PIECE OF THICK RED PAPER • STRING
SCISSORS • HOLE PUNCH
PAINTBRUSH AND PAINTS
MARKER PEN

1

Fold the paper in half lengthways. Make a fold on one side, about 1 in (2 cm) from the central fold.

2

Repeat this on the other side, so that the paper looks like a "W." The folds act as the floor of the canoe.

3

Keeping the folds pointing down, draw a canoe shape onto the side of the paper. Cut out the canoe.

4

Punch holes in the canoe's end. Tie the ends together using string. Push down the folds for the canoe's floor.

5

Use the paintbrush and paints to decorate your canoe.

Native North American canoes were made of bark wrapped around a wooden frame.
▼

When the Europeans first arrived, there were many tribes living in the southeast, including the Cherokee, the Chickasaw, the Creek, and the Seminole. These tribes lived in large settlements and were very successful farmers, growing corn and potatoes. Many people lived in round houses called "wigwams," which were made from logs covered in grass.

◄ Wigwams had a curved shape to let the rain run off.

GREEN CORN FESTIVAL

In the autumn, the tribes of the southeast celebrated the Green Corn Festival. The festival was held to thank the Spirit World for the harvest. Corn would be **sacrificed** to the spirits and there would be lots of dancing and music. The tribes would play drums, made from deerskin stretched across a hollow log, and shake rattles.

DID YOU KNOW?

NATIVE NORTH AMERICANS INVENTED THE GAME NOW CALLED LACROSSE. THEY CALLED IT "BAGGATAWAY." IN THE NATIVE NORTH AMERICAN VERSION, TEAMS COULD HAVE MORE THAN A HUNDRED MEMBERS.

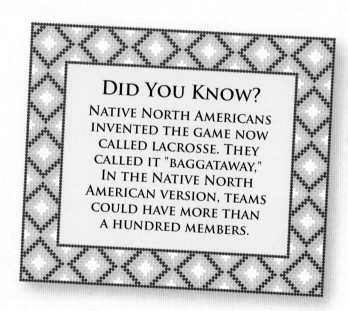

STAND OF THE SEMINOLE

When the USA was created in the 18th century, many of the southeast tribes were forced to move to new homes in the center of the country. One tribe, the Seminole, refused to go. Instead the tribe went to Florida. There, they fought many battles against the US army, which was unable to defeat them. Eventually, the US government decided to let them stay.

◄ Wooden rattles were often used at healing ceremonies to ward off evil spirits.

MAKE A RATTLE

Native North American rattles are made out of gourd fruits that have been hollowed out and dried.

YOU WILL NEED
THICK CARDSTOCK • BALLOON
NEWSPAPER • SCISSORS • PIN
STICKY TAPE • WHITE SCHOOL
GLUE MIXTURE (3 PARTS GLUE, 1
PART WATER) • PAINTBRUSH AND
PAINTS • DRIED BEANS • FUNNEL

1 Blow up the balloon and apply layers of newspaper strips and glue to the whole balloon, except the end.

2 When dry, pop the balloon. This is the rattle head.

3 Insert the funnel into the hole. Half fill the rattle head with the beans. Tape over the hole.

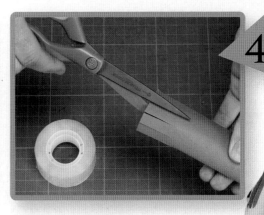

4 Roll up the cardstock and stick in place. Cut small slits at the top and fold down the flaps.

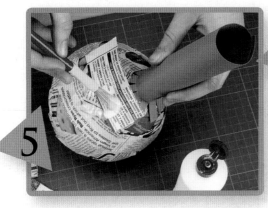

5 Glue the handle to your rattle head. Apply newspaper strips and glue to the join to make it stronger.

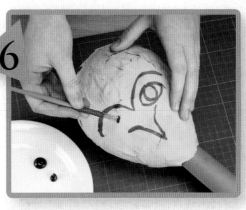

6 Use paints to decorate the rattle.

You could decorate your rattle with a picture of an animal spirit. ▶

15

LIFE ON THE GREAT PLAINS

The Great Plains is a massive grassy area that stretches across the center of North America. Before the Europeans arrived, the plains were home to vast herds of buffalo, which were hunted by the Native North American tribes. The tribes needed the buffalo for everything. Buffalo meat was the tribe's main source of food, their hides were used to make clothes and teepees, and the horns were turned into tools.

On the plains, hunters on horseback killed buffalo using bows and arrows.

HUNTING

To start with, Native North Americans hunted the buffalo on foot. However, in the 18th century, they began riding horses brought to the continent by Europeans. They soon became skilled riders, which made it much easier for them to follow the herds. The Europeans also introduced guns to North America, which the tribes used instead of bows and arrows.

The tribes lived in tents called teepees, made from wooden poles covered in buffalo hides.

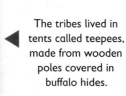

DID YOU KNOW?
BUFFALO WERE NOT ENTIRELY WIPED OUT IN NORTH AMERICA. SOME HAVE BEEN BRED IN CAPTIVITY, WHICH HAS HELPED TO INCREASE BUFFALO NUMBERS.

BUFFALO

In 1800, there may have been more than 100 million buffalo living on the Great Plains. About 80 years later, almost all of them had been killed. The US government wanted to force the Native North Americans off the plains, so they could use it for farmland and new towns. They thought that if they killed all the buffalo, the tribes would move.

MAKE A TEEPEE

The tribes used teepees because they could be put up and taken down very quickly as they followed the herds around.

YOU WILL NEED
FOUR THIN PIECES OF WOOD, EACH 12 IN (30 CM) LONG
STRING • THICK BROWN PAPER • CARDSTOCK • PENCIL
SCISSORS • PAINTBRUSH AND PAINT • STICKY TAPE

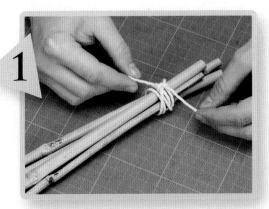

1

Gather the twigs in a bunch and loosely tie them together about 2 in (5 cm) from one end.

2

Stand the twigs in a triangle shape on the cardstock. Trace around it and cut out the shape.

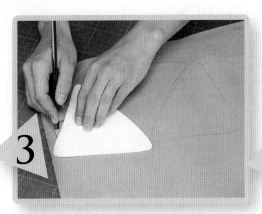

3

Using it as a template, draw five triangles next to each other on paper. Draw a door in one triangle.

4

Cut out the large shape and door. Fold along the triangle lines so you have a teepee shape.

5

Cut 2 in (5 cm) off the teepee top. Use paints to decorate your teepee.

Place the twigs inside the teepee and stick each twig to a different fold line. ▶

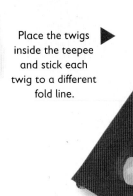

17

THE SIOUX

The Sioux (say *soo*) was one of the largest tribes living on the Great Plains. Throughout the 19th century, the tribe fought many battles against the US army, which was trying to take over its lands. In 1876, the Sioux warriors, led by Chief Sitting Bull, defeated General Custer and the US troops at the Battle of Little Big Horn—it is one of the most famous battles in US history.

Chief Sitting Bull was a leader and holy man of the Sioux in the late 19th century.

SCALPING

The tribes of the Great Plains fought many battles against each other. When one warrior defeated another, they would often take their scalp. To do this, the warrior cut away the skin and hair from the top of their enemy's head to show that they had been beaten.

Warriors of the Blackfoot and Sioux tribes fight on the Great Plains.

SUN DANCE

The Sioux's most important ceremony was the Sun Dance. It was performed at the start of each summer, before the first big buffalo hunt. The people of the tribe would sing, dance, and play drums. Sometimes the men danced for several days without food, water, or sleep, until they were exhausted. They believed that this brought them closer to the Spirit World.

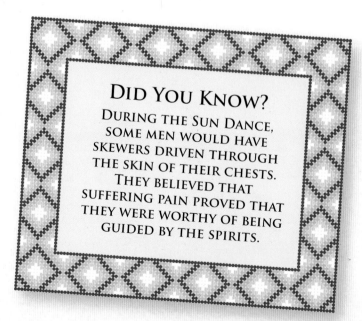

DID YOU KNOW?
DURING THE SUN DANCE, SOME MEN WOULD HAVE SKEWERS DRIVEN THROUGH THE SKIN OF THEIR CHESTS. THEY BELIEVED THAT SUFFERING PAIN PROVED THAT THEY WERE WORTHY OF BEING GUIDED BY THE SPIRITS.

MAKE A BUFFALO HIDE PICTURE STORY

Most Native North American tribes did not have a written language. Instead they would use pictures to tell stories.

YOU WILL NEED
BROWN PAPER • MARKER PEN
PAINTBRUSH AND PAINTS
SCISSORS

▲ This 19th-century Sioux buffalo blanket is decorated with pictures of the tribe's legends.

1 Crumple the brown paper, then smooth it out, so that it looks like animal skin.

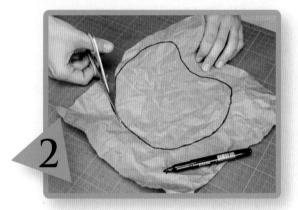

2 Draw and cut out a shape from the paper.

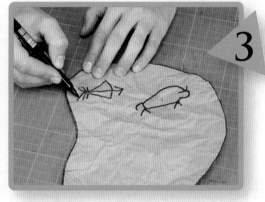

3 Draw symbols such as a buffalo or a bow and arrow to make a story or message.

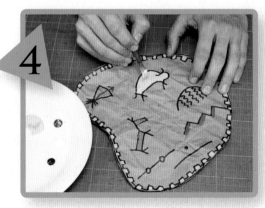

4 Use paints to color in the symbols and to draw a border around your picture story.

Some tribes used buffalo hides to record their history. ▶

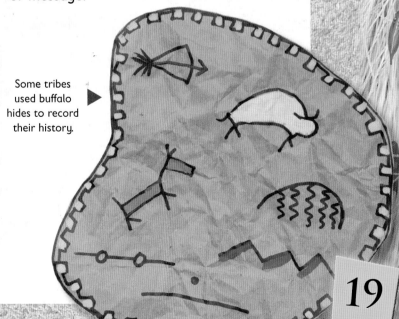

19

The Southwest

▲

This pueblo village, called the Cliff Palace, was carved out of the rock 1,000 years ago.

Much of the American southwest is covered by desert. The people who lived there became experts at **irrigation** —carefully using the little water there was to grow crops. Each year, they performed the Snake Ceremony, when they would pray to the spirits for rain. The tribes lived in settlements that Spanish explorers called pueblos (which means towns), so the tribes became known as the pueblo people. Many of the tribes in this region, including the Hopi and the Zuni, have lived there for thousands of years.

Hogans were perfect desert homes —cool in the day and warm at night.

▼

CALIFORNIAN GOLD RUSH

In the woods and forests of California, the tribes lived by hunting and fishing. The first Europeans did not arrive in this area until the late 18th century. To begin with, the tribes and settlers lived together peacefully. Then in 1848, gold was discovered. Over the next few years thousands of people arrived hoping to make their fortune. This forced the Native North Americans to move elsewhere.

A modern copy of a traditional coil pot. ▶

THE NAVAJO

The Navajo were one of the most famous tribes in the southwest. They lived in roundhouses made from wood and clay called hogans, and stored food in clay coil pots. They were brave warriors and skilled farmers. They used sheep's wool to make clothes, which they traded.

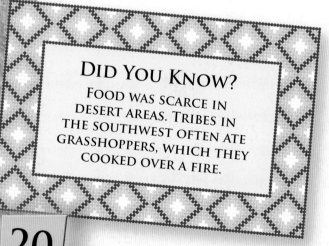

DID YOU KNOW?
FOOD WAS SCARCE IN DESERT AREAS. TRIBES IN THE SOUTHWEST OFTEN ATE GRASSHOPPERS, WHICH THEY COOKED OVER A FIRE.

MAKE A COIL POT

Tribes in the southwest made pots using long coils of clay stuck one on top of the other.

YOU WILL NEED
MODELING CLAY
PAIR OF COMPASSES
PENCIL

Roll out a flat piece of clay. Use a pair of compasses to mark a circle about 4 in (10 cm) wide.

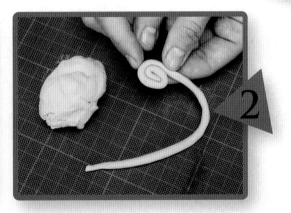

Roll out a long thin sausage of clay and bend it into a coil.

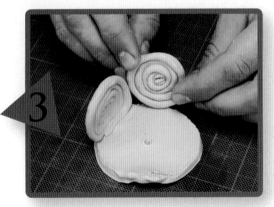

Press the coil into the edge of your circle. Roll out another coil of clay and add it next to the first.

Add coils, spirals and beads of clay until your pot is 4 in (10 cm) high.

Make sure you pinch together any gaps in your pot. Leave to dry.

▶ You could use your pot to store pens and pencils.

LIFE IN THE NORTHWEST

The northwest was home to one of most amazing Native North American cultures. Here, about 30 tribes lived in the thick forests. There was so much food available in these forests that the tribes had plenty of spare time to practice arts and crafts. These tribes are well known for their giant wooden sculptures, called "totem poles."

◀ Every totem pole had a different design.

▲ Masks were used by the Kwakiutl tribe in their ceremonies.

MASKED DANCERS

The tribes of the northwest performed ceremonies in which the dancers would act out stories. The dancers wore carved masks in the shape of spirits and would shake wooden rattles.

DID YOU KNOW?

TOTEM POLES COULD BE MORE THAN 40 FEET (12 METERS) HIGH. THEY WERE DECORATED WITH PICTURES OF SPIRITS, OFTEN IN THE FORM OF ANIMALS, SUCH AS EAGLES, BEARS AND WOLVES.

POTLATCH

One of the region's most important ceremonies was potlatch. During a potlatch, the richest members of the tribe would give away gifts and money to poorer members. Then there was a large feast. Potlatches are still held today.

MAKE A TOTEM POLE

A totem pole showed a family's importance and power. They were also a way of remembering the dead.

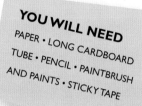

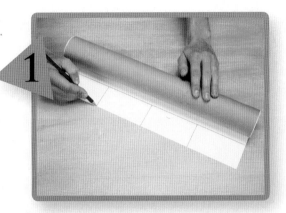

1 Measure a piece of paper the same length as the tube. Divide it into four parts.

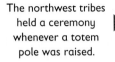
The northwest tribes held a ceremony whenever a totem pole was raised. ▶

YOU WILL NEED
PAPER · LONG CARDBOARD TUBE · PENCIL · PAINTBRUSH AND PAINTS · STICKY TAPE

2 In each piece, draw an animal face, one on top of the other. Make the top animal an eagle.

3 Cut out the strip. Use paints to color in the animals' faces.

4 Wrap the paper around the cardboard tube and stick it in position using sticky tape.

5 Draw, color, and cut out some wings for the eagle. Stick to the back of the totem pole.

LIFE IN THE FROZEN NORTH

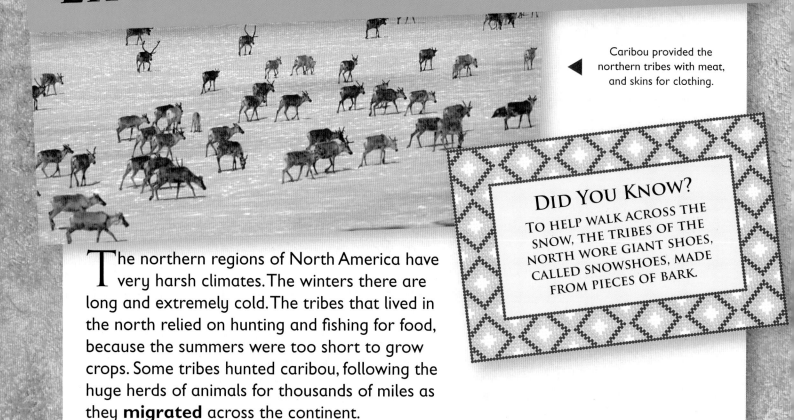

Caribou provided the northern tribes with meat, and skins for clothing.

The northern regions of North America have very harsh climates. The winters there are long and extremely cold. The tribes that lived in the north relied on hunting and fishing for food, because the summers were too short to grow crops. Some tribes hunted caribou, following the huge herds of animals for thousands of miles as they **migrated** across the continent.

The Inuit wore the furs of animals, which they hunted using **harpoons**.

GETTING AROUND
The tribes in this region traveled using sleds pulled by teams of dogs. These sleds could go very fast. To travel across the sea, the tribes made **kayaks** using the skins of animals stretched across wooden frames.

INUIT
The Inuit people are believed to have arrived in North America much later than the other Native North American tribes. They settled on the freezing shores of the Arctic Ocean, hunting large animals that could provide a lot of meat, such as seals and whales. They built their homes in round igloos, made of ice.

Lamps were used to melt the igloo ice slightly, which helped to stick the blocks together.

24

MAKE AN IGLOO

The Inuit people made houses called igloos using blocks of snow. They were warm and cozy inside.

YOU WILL NEED
MODELING CLAY • SMALL BALL
• MODELING TOOL PAINTBRUSH
AND WHITE PAINT

Wrap the clay around the ball so that it covers just over half of its surface.

Use the modeling tool to cut away extra clay so there is an exact half-ball-sized piece. Remove the ball.

Use the modeling tool to draw the shape of blocks on the outside of the half ball. This is the igloo.

Cut a small hole in the side of the igloo. Place an arch-shaped piece over this entrance to the igloo.

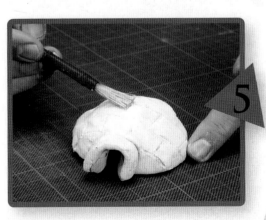

Leave the clay to dry and then paint it white.

The Inuit built large igloos with many rooms for lots of people. ▶

25

LIFE WITH THE EUROPEAN SETTLERS

Europeans began arriving in North America in the 16th century. As the years went by, the situation between the new settlers and the Native North Americans grew worse. To begin with, the two peoples were able to live together peacefully. However, as time passed, the two sides began to fight over land. Gradually the entire continent was taken over by the settlers and two huge new countries were created—the USA and Canada.

Native North American warriors and US troops fought at the Battle of Tippecanoe in 1811.

THE "INDIAN WARS"

In the 19th century, the USA began to take over more and more land. Many tribes were forced to move from their lands to new homes called reservations. Several battles between Native North American tribes and the US Army were fought. These were known as the "Indian Wars." Eventually, the Native North Americans were beaten.

◀ Native North Americans made traditional crafts, such as these Kachina dolls.

THANKSGIVING

The US and Canadian festival of Thanksgiving celebrates a time when the Native North Americans and Europeans lived peacefully with each other. A Native North American tribe gave some settlers food to survive the winter and showed them how to farm. The settlers gave a festival of thanks in return.

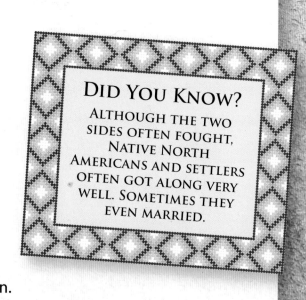

DID YOU KNOW?
ALTHOUGH THE TWO SIDES OFTEN FOUGHT, NATIVE NORTH AMERICANS AND SETTLERS OFTEN GOT ALONG VERY WELL. SOMETIMES THEY EVEN MARRIED.

MAKE AN EAGLE SPIRIT KACHINA DOLL

Kachina dolls were created to look like spirits. The dolls taught Native North American children about religion and the Spirit World.

YOU WILL NEED
CARDBOARD TUBE • COTTON BALLS • CARDSTOCK • SCISSORS STICKY TAPE • PAINTBRUSH AND PAINTS • PIECE OF FABRIC • MARKER PEN RULER • GLUE

1 Cut two 1.5 in (4 cm) by 1.5 in (4 cm) "T" shapes, one at the back and one at the front of the cardboard roll.

2 Curl the flaps to form two tubes for legs. Stick together. Cut out eagle claws from cardstock. Stick on.

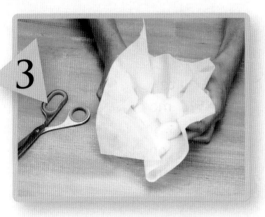

3 Tie the cotton balls up inside a piece of fabric to make a big ball for the head.

4 Make a beak from cardstock and stick it on the head. Paint eyes and feathers. Push the head into the tube.

5 Paint and cut out the wings from a piece of cardstock. Stick them to back of the tube. Decorate with paints.

Your doll stands for an eagle spirit. ► There were about 400 different types of Kachina doll.

27

NATIVE NORTH AMERICANS TODAY

Today there are many Native North Americans living in the USA and Canada. The USA has more than 500 Native North American **reservations** and Canada has more than 300 First Nation **reserves**. These areas are governed by the tribal people living there. Many Native North Americans also live outside these areas in American and Canadian towns. There are believed to be around three million Native North American people in North America.

◄ Astronaut John Herrington was the first Native North American to travel into space.

RESERVATION LIFE
On reservations and reserves, Native North Americans practice their traditional ways of life. They speak their own languages, wear traditional clothes, perform native dances, and play games.

Dancing at a traditional powwow festival.
▼

DID YOU KNOW?
TODAY, NATIVE NORTH AMERICAN TRIBES GET TOGETHER FOR CELEBRATIONS CALLED POWWOWS, WHEN THEY SING, DANCE, AND WEAR TRADITIONAL COSTUMES.

Some reservations operate successful **casinos**, which are not common in the rest of the USA.
▼

THE NAVAJO
The largest Native North American reservation in North America is the 15-million-acre Navajo reservation in Arizona. Most of the people there speak both the Navajo language and English.

28

PLAY A NATIVE NORTH AMERICAN CHANCE GAME

Games were popular with Native North American tribes throughout North America.

YOU WILL NEED
THICK CARDSTOCK • PENCIL
PAIR OF COMPASSES • SCISSORS
MARKER PEN

1 Draw five circles on the cardstock, each 1.5 in (4 cm) wide. Cut them out. These are your counters.

2 On two of the counters, draw a picture of an eagle on one side. Leave the other side blank.

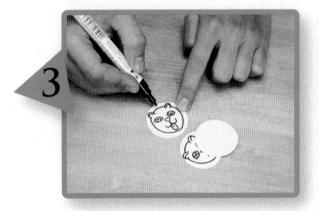

3 On the other three counters, draw a picture of a bear on one side. Leave the other side blank.

4 To play, throw the counters in the air. You get different points for the different animals showing.

5 The first person to reach 50 points wins.

RULES FOR TWO PLAYERS

THE SCORING:

Blank	0 points
Bear	1 point
Eagle	2 points

29

GLOSSARY

Calumet A long pipe for smoking tobacco. Also known as a peace pipe.

Caribou A type of North American deer that lives in large herds. Also known as a reindeer.

Casino A place where gambling games take place.

Ceremony An occasion, usually involving singing and dancing, when Native North Americans ask their gods for help.

Harpoon A weapon used for hunting.

Ice Age A time, many thousands of years ago, when the Earth's water froze and sea levels fell, leaving behind a bridge of land between Northeast Asia and Northwest America.

Immune To not be affected by a particular disease or illness.

Irrigation Watering farmland, usually by getting the water to flow into fields along a series of small canals.

Kayak A type of lightweight canoe.

Migrate To move from one region to another, often in search of food.

Nomads People who have no permanent home, but travel from place to place.

Powwow A traditional Native North American ceremony, usually involving a feast, singing, and dancing.

Reservation An area of land within the United States where Native North Americans live.

Reserve An area of land within Canada where Native North Americans live.

Sacrifice To give away something valuable in order to please a spirit, god, or gods.

Tribe A group of people who have the same beliefs and language. They usually live in an area, ruled by a leader.

Worship To pray or perform a religious ceremony in honor of a god or holy spirit.

NOTES FOR PARENTS AND TEACHERS

- View factsheets about Native North American food, clothing, hairstyles, and homes, and read about the many different tribes—from the Alenakis to the Zunis—at http://www.native-languages.org/kids.htm.

- Making dolls from corn husks (the leaves surrounding an ear of corn) has long been a popular Native North American craft. Buy a bag of husks and get the children to have a go at making their own dolls. You can print out instructions from www.teachersfirst.com/summer/cornhusk.htm. For more on the different types, uses, and meanings of dolls, go to www.native-languages.org/dolls.htm.

- Explore the various Native North American regions on the clickable map at www.ahsd25.k12.il.us/Curriculum Info/NativeAmericans/index.html. You can also read about the myths, legends, and stories associated with these areas at http://www.kstrom.net/isk/stories/SEmyths.html. Ask the children to do a project on their favorite Native North American story.

- Log on to warrensburg.k12.mo.us/iadventure/nativeam/ to go on an interactive adventure through 18th-century North America. You follow the journey of an 11-year-old child from London, England, who has arrived in North America.

- At http://americanart.si.edu/exhibitions/online/catlinclassroom/, a virtual presentation by the Smithsonian Museum, you can listen to the stories of George Caitlin. He was an American artist who spent the 1830s visiting more than 140 Native North American tribes, painting and writing about them.

Useful websites

- Design a virtual wampum belt, play an Ojibwa language game, and learn about traditional Native North American toys at www.nativetech.org/games/index.php.

- Read about some of the greatest Native North American leaders, chiefs, and heroes from history at www.indigenouspeople.net/leaders.htm, and then learn about the lives of ten modern Native North Americans at www.manataka.org/page136.html.

- Explore the online collection of the National Museum of the American Indian at www.nmai.si.edu.

- Browse the photographs from the Native North American section of the Library of Congress's "American Memory" collection at http://memory.loc.gov/ammem/index.html.